CW00502439

This book is only made possible by the genius of Theodor Seuss Geisel, aka Dr Seuss, who first opened my doors of perception. By parodying him and attempting to stick to his rules I am even more in love with and in awe of his mind-bending original book.

Geoff Allnutt

This edition published by Burning Eye Books 2015

www.burningeye.co.uk

@burningeyebooks

Burning Eye Books
15 West Hill, Portishead, BS20 6LG

ISBN 978 1 90913 6 663

The fridge did not work.

We were too skint to eat.

So we smoked in the lounge

Like our fags were a teat.

1

I smoked with my Mandy.

We smoked to bring cheer.

And I said, "God I wish

That our birthdays were near!"

Too skint to go out

And too skint to drink beer.

So we smoked in the lounge.

We did little but sneer.

2

So all we could do was to
Smoke!

    Smoke!

        Smoke!

            Smoke!

And we could not stand it.

Us both being broke.

Then our

Doorbell was pressed!

How that press made us stressed!

We hid!

When we heard him ask us for a chat!

We hid!

When we heard him!

The Twat from the flat!

When he banged our door

Flat, with his rat a tat tat!

6

"I heard you were skint
And the rent is still owing.
But we can get high
If you come where I'm going!"

7

"I have some great gear we could try,"
Said the Twat.
"I have some Red Leb,"
Said the Twat in our flat.
"A ton of pink pills,
I will share them with you.
Your landlord
Will not care at all if I do."

Poor Mandy and I
We just sat in our chairs.
Our landlord had gone to his church
for his prayers.

8

But our roach said, "No Way!
Make that Twat go upstairs!
Tell the Twat in our flat
You do NOT want his wares.
You should not get stoned.
You don't need his support.
You should not get stoned
When your landlord is short!"

11

"Now! Now! Have no qualms.

Have no qualms!" said the Twat.

"My pills are not bad,"

Said the Twat in our flat.

"Why, we can take

Lots of great drugs, if you dare,

With a line at a time

Up your snout like a hare!"

"Put them down!" said the roach.

"This is not to be tried!"

"Put them down!" said the roach.

"I do NOT wish to chide!"

13

"Have no qualms!" said the Twat.

"For the drugs must be tried.

I will get you so high

That your brains will be fried.

With a beer in one hand!

And my tongue on some khat!

But that is not ALL I can down!"

Said the Twat...

14

"Down!

Get them down!

Get them down!" said the Twat

With his tongue round an E

And on top of the khat!

"I can down two MORE beers!

I can smoke up this roach!

And a double malt scotch!

And some weed I can poach!

And look!

I can go up and down with this speed,

And look!

How I laugh right out loud on this weed!"

16

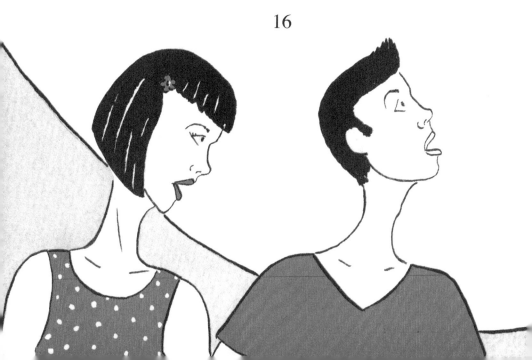

"Down!

Get them down!

Get them down!" said the Twat.

"It is fun to take drugs."

And he sung out in scat,

"I can get down the speed

And the weed and the E!

I can neck down three beers!

And a roach on this spree!

I can down a malt scotch

And a double neat gin!

And in my big gob

I can smoke up this skin!

I can smoke up the skin

As I whizz on the speed!

And look how I laugh

Right out

Loud, on this weed..."

18

And the Twat looked a sight...

As his face it went white!

He crashed down with a thump

From the strength of the weed.

And Mandy and I,

We heard the Twat's voice plead!

21

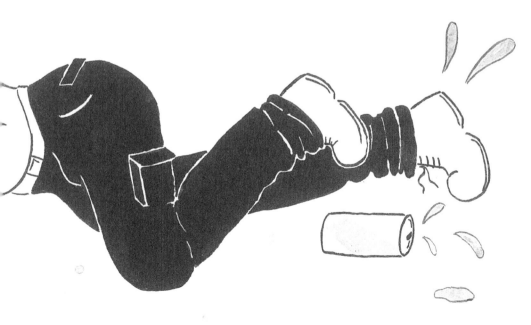

And our roach cried out, too.

In an ashtray he sat!

He said, "I can not laugh

Out loud, at this Twat.

This is not some good gear,"

Said our roach as he smoked,

As he filled up his lungs,

And then quietly choked!

22

"Now look what you did!"

Croaked the roach to the Twat.

"Just look at this lounge!

Look at this! Look at that!

You downed the malt scotch,

Downed it quick with an E.

You messed up our lounge

When you went on this spree

You SHOULD NOT get stoned

When their landlord is out.

Now get out of this flat!"

Said the roach with a shout.

25

"But I like to do drugs.

Look, I have to come out!"

Said the Twat in our flat

To the roach with a pout.

"I will NOT smoke solo,

When I HAVE spliff to share!

There's spare!" said the Twat. "In my flat,

Spare

    Spare

        Spare...

I will give you

Narcotics and drugs that are rare!"

27

And then he slipped out.
And, then, quick as a flash,
The Twat from the flat
Came back in with a crash.

28

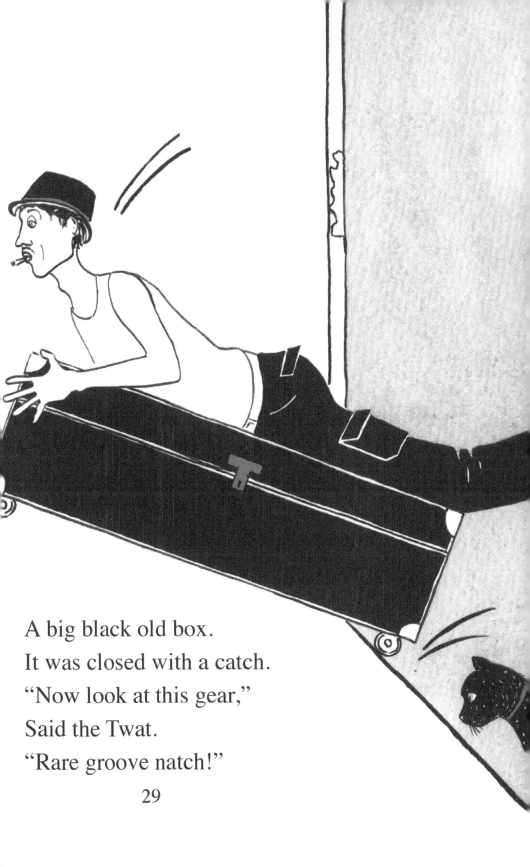

A big black old box.
It was closed with a catch.
"Now look at this gear,"
Said the Twat.
"Rare groove natch!"

29

Then he flipped up the catch

On the box that was matt.

"I call this game SCRATCH WITH A CATCH,"

Said the Twat.

"In this box are two decks

I will play for your soul.

I can mix these two decks,"

Said the Twat on a roll.

31

"I will mash up these tracks.
You will hear something new.
From decks that I scratch on
Deck One and Deck Two.
These Decks they will move you,
And, when you take drugs
You're out of your box
And the room fills with hugs!"
Then he plugged in the Decks
And said, "You are my crew.
Would you like to mix tracks
On Deck One and Deck Two?"

33

Poor Mandy and I

We just sat in our seats

As he mixed up two tracks,

Filled the lounge up with beats.

He mixed the two decks,

But our roach said, "No Way!

These decks should not spin

At this time! Of the day!"

34

"He should not mix tracks

When your landlord is short!

Turn them down! Turn them down!"

Said the roach with a snort.

35

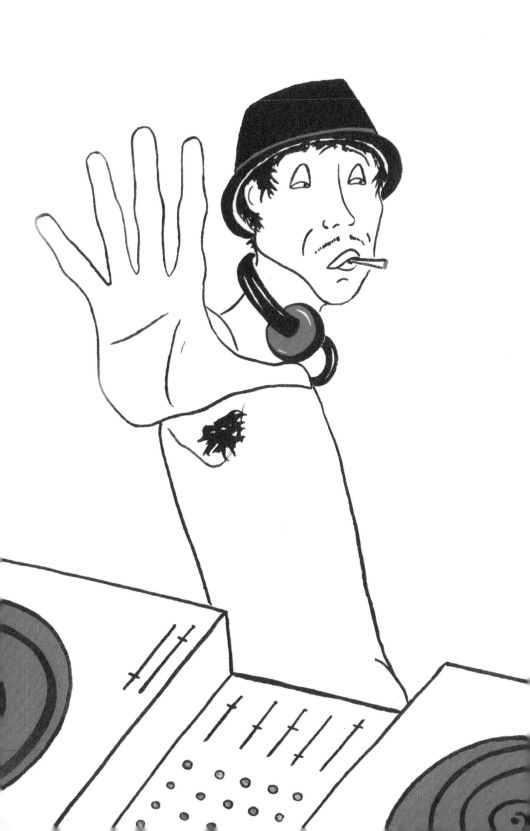

"Have no qualms, silly roach,"
Said the Twat in our flat.
"These tracks are great tracks.
They are hot, they are phat.
They are great. Oh, so great!
Let us dance to the beat.
We can dance and take drugs,
Drink and smoke, and not eat."

37

"Now here is a groove that I like,"
Said the Twat.
"I want to dance now,"
Said the Twat in our flat.

38

"No! Not in the lounge!"

Said the roach with a snort.

"You should not dance now

In the lounge! For your sport!

Oh, the tracks you will play!

Oh, the tracks you will mix!

You're too stoned to do it!

And one needle sticks!"

39

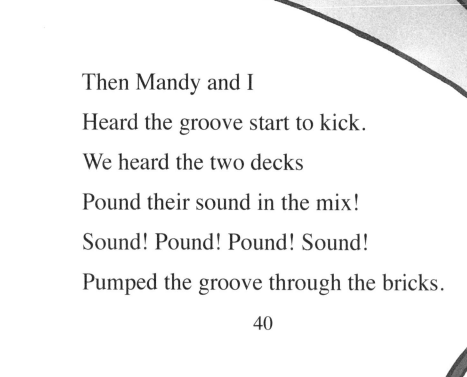

Then Mandy and I

Heard the groove start to kick.

We heard the two decks

Pound their sound in the mix!

Sound! Pound! Pound! Sound!

Pumped the groove through the bricks.

40

Deck One and Deck Two!
Pumped the groove! Through the flat!
Through the sound of the decks
Purred our landlord's black cat!
Who danced as he downed
Some pink pills, off the Twat.
Then we saw the old cat
Lose his mind on the mat!

Then we saw his highness

Chop up two lines and snort,

And then down two more beers

And a glass of old port.

And I said,

"I do NOT like the way that you mix!

Our landlord has paid,

And worked hard for these bricks!"

45

Then our roach said, "Look Out!"

And our roach he turned grey.

"Your landlord is on his way back

For his pay!

Oh, what will he do to us?

What will he say?

Oh, he will not like it

Let's all of us pray!"

"So DO something! Quick!" said the roach.
"Try to think!

And pour out your landlord,
Your landlord a drink!
So, as quick as you can,
Or your landlord will sue,
You will have to get rid of
Deck One and Deck Two!"

48

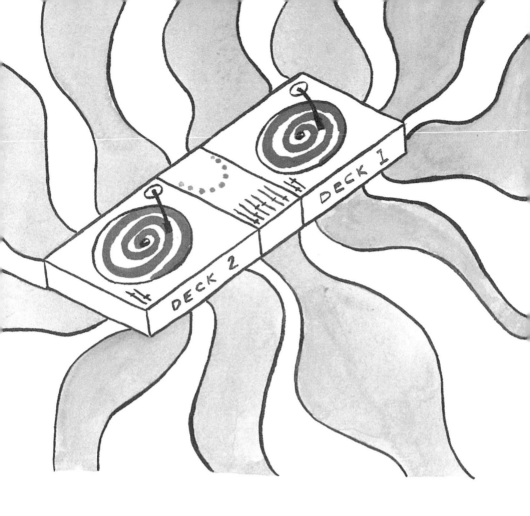

So, as quick as I could,

I then lifted our throw.

And I said, "With this throw

I can hide them I know.

I know, with my throw,

I can clean like a pro!"

Then I threw down my throw.

It flew fast with a glide,

And I killed them! At last!

The two decks they had FRIED!

Then I said to the Twat,

As we picked up our chairs,

"You pick up these Decks

And you take them upstairs!"

"Oh no!" said the Twat.

"You do not like my wares...

Oh no.

Not the stairs!

Not the stairs!

Not the stairs!"

53

Then he closed up the decks

In the box with the catch.

And the Twat went upstairs

With a no smoking patch.

54

"That is great," said the roach.

"He has gone upstairs. Great.

But your landlord will see.

He will see just you wait!

And the drugs are so strong

And so thick is the smoke,

If he's back at the flat,

He could well have a stroke!"

55

And THEN!

Who was back in the lounge?

Why, the Twat!

"Have no fear of the gear,"

Said the Twat from the flat.

"I always knock back all the empties

With flair...

I will neck these narcotics

And drugs that are rare!"

57

Then we saw him neck back

All the drugs that were out.

He necked back the scotch,

And the coke up his snout,

And the khat, and the beers,

And the weed he could poach,

And the gin, and the speed,

And the pills and his roach.

He necked one last double.

Then he said, "That is that."

And then he was gone

The Twat from our flat.

Then our landlord came back
And he asked for a smoke,
"Do you have any cash?"
He said that for a joke.

And Mandy and I, we just sat
In our chairs,
And we told him
That soon God would hear our poor prayers.

We lied, said the money

It was due to be through!

Well...

What would YOU do

If your landlord asked you?

61

Thank You

We would like to give a big 'thank you' to all the people who encouraged and assisted us in getting this project off the ground:

Patience Agbabi, Clive Birnie, Will Buchanan, Lucy English, Katie Glover, Rosemary Harris, Sarah Higbee, Julia Hughes, Philip Jeays, Sue Jenkins, Audi Maserati, Jonah Munn, Ludo Munn, Ursula Munn, Sarah Palmer, Caroline Sutton, William Sutton, Steve Tasane and Debbie Watkins.

Geoff Allnutt and Annabel Munn

Geoff Allnutt, aka The Speech Painter, has been a performance poet since 1988. He has performed all over the UK from poetry clubs to music and literature festivals and is the winner of numerous poetry slams (including Glastonbury Festival). His verse play, *Walt Disney, Man or Mouse?*, premiered at Apples & Snakes in 1994. Between 1995 and 1998 he was a founder-member of poetry's first pop group, Atomic Lip, together with Patience Agbabi, Steve Tasane, Pink Sly and Joelle Taylor. He staged his first one man show, *Beating Time*, in 2000 and, in 2003, he was co-host and co-programmer for *Pure Poetry* at Soho Theatre, a weekly poetry cabaret show placing page poets and performance poets together on the same stage. His film poem, *This Time Next Year*, was commissioned for Channel 4 in 2004 and he is also a regular support act for chanson singer Philip Jeays. 2011 saw Geoff commissioned to write and perform at a celebration in recognition of the poets and writers Alice and Wilfred Meynells and the centenary of their house purchase in Greatham, Sussex. In 2014, alongside Will Buchanan and Kylie Earl, he finally formed his first band Radio K W G and is their lyricist, backing vocalist and harmonica player. Radio K W G has released two EPs and is currently working on a third.

speechpainter.com

Annabel Munn has worked and exhibited as a ceramic artist, sculptor, painter and illustrator for over twenty years. As well as featuring in many group exhibitions she has had a number of one-woman shows and now works mainly to commission. Her work has appeared in furniture magazines and lifestyle and interiors magazines such as *Mines and West Furniture Launch*, *SQ2*, *World of Interiors*, *Interiors*, and more. Annabel's work can be found in private collections across Europe and the USA, as well as in the *W A Ismay Collection*, Yorkshire Museum. She set up Peter's Barn Gallery in Sussex and curated their collections for over ten years. She was invited to and worked at the UWE Enamelling Research Programme in Bristol. She now teaches regularly and is frequently on judging panels for Art and Craft Exhibitions. Publications: *The Tile*, by Kenneth Clarke, MBE; *A History of 20th Century British Tiles*, by Chris Blanchett. Recent work: Annabel has written and illustrated two books for children, created a bronze memorial sculpture, developed a logo for avant-garde circus company Pirates of the Carabina and is currently designing posters and artwork for their new show *Flown*. Two of Annabel's tile designs have even been made into tattoos, resulting in requests for two more tattoo designs!

annabelmunn.com

Lightning Source UK Ltd.
Milton Keynes UK
UKOW07f0537201015

260975UK00010B/32/P